JADEN ANGELES

Simple Investing Hacks: Gen Z Edition

Easy, simplified ways you can start investing in your 20's

Copyright © 2024 by jaden angeles

All rights reserved. No part of this publication may be reproduced, stored or transmitted in any form or by any means, electronic, mechanical, photocopying, recording, scanning, or otherwise without written permission from the publisher. It is illegal to copy this book, post it to a website, or distribute it by any other means without permission.

jaden angeles asserts the moral right to be identified as the author of this work.

jaden angeles has no responsibility for the persistence or accuracy of URLs for external or third-party Internet Websites referred to in this publication and does not guarantee that any content on such Websites is, or will remain, accurate or appropriate.

Designations used by companies to distinguish their products are often claimed as trademarks. All brand names and product names used in this book and on its cover are trade names, service marks, trademarks and registered trademarks of their respective owners. The publishers and the book are not associated with any product or vendor mentioned in this book. None of the companies referenced within the book have endorsed the book.

First edition

This book was professionally typeset on Reedsy.
Find out more at reedsy.com

Contents

Introduction		1
1	Hack #1 - Open A High Yield Savings Account	4
2	Hack #2 - Contribute to a 401(k)	8
3	Hack #3 - Open a Roth IRA	11
4	Hack #4 - Open a Health Savings Account (optional)	16
5	Hack #5 - Compound Interest is on our side	18
6	Hack #6 - Investing in Yourself!	20
7	Conclusion	23
8	References	25

Introduction

I'm Gen Z. I was born in 1998, I live in the Bay Area, and I'm struggling to find time for my hobbies outside of my first full-time job. I wake up early and work for 8 hours, dealing with traffic, feeling tired after working, and finding motivation to do something at home other than scroll on my phone while I fall asleep wasting my precious free time.

I'm Gen Z. I was born with the internet, I constantly help my parents with their phone or their computer. I have access to the knowledge of anything and everything through the internet, yet I use my time to watch videos on social media and take pictures of my dog to send to my friends.

I'm Gen Z. Up until last year, I had no idea that I could be making and saving money and that if I let it sit there, I could potentially become a millionaire by the time I retire all while still scrolling on my phone wasting my free time playing video games.

If this sounds like you, and you want to learn simple ways you can invest your money to make it work for you then you have come to the right place. As a member of Gen Z, I personally know what it's like to feel like to be in the dark about retirement. I have so many years until I need to worry about that, so why would I worry now? The answer is simple: If you start now, then time is on your side and compound interest will be in your favor. If you have no idea what that means, don't worry I got you, basically your money will grow as time passes. This is important because as people of Gen Z, we have nothing but time on our side. We spend so much time scrolling, playing video games, watching t.v. shows, movies, and streams. What more could we want but to spend that time doing the same things but also making money from it? Not only that, but you could be growing your money without having to manage it everyday: it will grow on its own. All you have to do is add money and watch it grow throughout the years. Gen Z needs to do this now because although we have time on our side right now, that won't be the case in 5 years.

In this book, I want to highlight some key investing hacks that are so low maintenance that people like me, who want to do the bare minimum, can benefit. The word investing is scary, because a lot of us don't really know the definition of it. Luckily, these simple hacks will allow you to first, understand in simple terms what it means to invest, and second, tell you exactly where and what to invest in so that all you have to do is let your money sit and let time do the work.

For the purpose of this book, I want to emphasize that the only things that are required to follow these simple hacks are:

- A Bank Account
- Source of Income
- Phone/Laptop

These hacks are just a few of the ways you can begin investing and not have it be as daunting as you first believe it is. You will also benefit from these hacks, simply because it is coming from someone like you, a Gen Z who just recently got their first full-time job with no prior knowledge of what it means to invest. With that, here are simple investing hacks for

INTRODUCTION

Gen Z.

1

Hack #1 - Open A High Yield Savings Account

This first hack is very simple. If you have a job, or another source of income, then you must also have a bank account. Now if you are like me, then most likely it was your parents who opened up your first bank account and gave you your first debit card. You've been using it for years because that's all you knew and you don't know that you can actually switch banks to basically get free money.

What is a High Yield Savings Account?

Simply put, a high yield savings account is a type of savings account that has an annual percentage yield (AYP) that is above average. Annual percentage yield, or APY for short, is basically how much interest you can earn from putting your money into a savings account. The higher the percentage, the faster the rate of return your money gets in your bank account. Here is a simple example:

Fred puts $100 into his savings account that has an APY of 5%. His savings account is compounded monthly, meaning that at the beginning of each month his $100 accrues interest. At the end of the year, Fred's

HACK #1 - OPEN A HIGH YIELD SAVINGS ACCOUNT

$100 increases to $105 because of the 5% apy.

Keep in mind that Fred didn't add any money to his savings account and he basically got that $5 for free. Although that does not seem like a big difference, you'd be surprised to see just how much you can earn if we apply this to real life. I can use myself as an example:

In October 2023, I moved all of my savings into a high yield savings account with an apy of about 5% at the time. Since then, the apy has gone down to 4.50% but even with the lowered apy, I accumulated over $900 in just one year simply by changing where I put my money.

Why do I need a High Yield Savings Account?

As you've read from my own personal example, I managed to literally get free money just from having my savings sit in a high yield savings account. Instead of having your money just sitting in your checking account or another savings account with little to no apy that your parents opened for you, it is the smart and efficient decision to invest into opening up a high yield savings account and putting your money in it. I will admit, it was tedious to move all of my money from one place to the next, but it is 100% worth it to invest in this as it has gotten me and many others free money without having to do anything.

Take my first bank account for example: my mom opened up my first college checking account with Chase back when I was just in high school. I put all of my money in there from when I was in college to my first job until last October of 2023. When you search up the apy for a Chase savings account, the apy is 0.01%. Another example, I know a lot of people who have savings in banks like Wells Fargo, or Bank of America, most likely because that is where their parents opened their first bank account. Unfortunately, the apy for Wells Fargo's Platinum Savings is 0.05% and Bank of America's Advantage savings is 0.04%. These savings accounts are probably the most popular but also the most sad to me because us Gen Z have no idea of the different types of savings accounts we could utilize and invest in, such as a high yield savings account.

HYS Recommendations

To make things very easy for you, here is a list of high yield savings accounts that I recommend. Please note, that although the higher the apy, they are subject to change so it is best to just pick one of these and stick to it, even if the apy isn't the highest that you will see.

- Capital One's 360 Performance Savings account with an apy of 3.80% as of December 12, 2024
- SoFi Savings account with an apy of 4% as of December 12, 2024
- American Express High Yield Savings account with an apy of 3.90% as of December 13, 2024

The high yield savings account that I personally use is Western Alliance Bank with an apy of 4.5% as of December 13, 2024. However, I recommend the three I listed because I know that they are more convenient, easier to withdraw from, and are more known banks than Western Alliance, which may feel more safe to others. That is not to say that Western Alliance Bank isn't trustworthy, as I have again accumulated about $900 since moving my money to their high yield savings account.

After you open up your high yield savings account, all you need to do

HACK #1 - OPEN A HIGH YIELD SAVINGS ACCOUNT

is add your money to it and let it grow. It is important to note that the more money you add to it, the faster it will grow. So don't let any extra money just sit in your checking account, invest into putting a portion of your paycheck into your savings account for that free money that can accumulate by just letting it sit there.

2

Hack #2 - Contribute to a 401(k)

When I started my first part-time job, I remember that we had a meeting with the owner about how he is making changes to the company. The change that I remember and still regret not taking advantage of, was that our company would now allow all employees, both part-time and full-time, to contribute to a 401k plan for employees 21 and over. At the time, I was only 19, not knowing what these terms were and I wasn't even at the age where I needed to know about this anyway so I accepted it and continued working. 5 years later, still working with that same company, I finally decided to enroll into the 401k plan. If I could turn back time, I would make sure that 21 year old me knew to enroll and contribute to a 401k right when I hit the right age.

Although this may be simple for some people, I know that if I didn't understand it at that age then there are others who also don't understand it. I am here to rescue those people of Gen Z and help them realize the mistake I made years ago, and the free money that I lost along the way.

What is a 401k?

HACK #2 - CONTRIBUTE TO A 401(K)

A 401k is a type of retirement account, usually offered by an employer, that lets you set aside part of your paycheck to invest for retirement. This is by far the most popular retirement account and yet when I was 19, I had no idea how big of an impact it can have on someone's future. From my experience it is one of, if not the most, easiest way to invest. You simply enroll in one with your employer, set a certain amount or percentage from your paycheck that you want to contribute, and then once you get your paycheck, part of it is automatically invested into your 401k.

Why you need to enroll in a 401k (if your employer provides it).

As I've mentioned, I failed to take advantage of enrolling into my employer's 401k plan once I was eligible. Do not make the same mistake as I did and make sure that if your job offers a 401k, to take advantage and invest part of your paycheck in it. Not only is it one of the easiest and low maintenance ways you can invest, but it's also a good way to save up for retirement. And again, to reiterate, I know that us Gen Z have nothing but time on our side so why is there a need to worry about saving up for retirement now? The answer is because since we have so much time, we can use that to our advantage and save ahead so that it isn't too late.

One of the biggest advantages to enrolling in a 401k with your employer, is if your employer offers an employee match or 401k match. A 401k match is when the employer also contributes money into your 401k based on how much money you yourself contributed. Each employer has different employee match rates, along with other qualifications for how much or when they contribute. If your employer offers a 401k match, it is essential that you are putting that to full use so that you can fully benefit from the match and get free money.

For example, if your employer offers a 100% match of what you contribute for up to 5% of your salary, this means that your employer will give you 5% of your salary if you also contribute up to 5%. To put it simply, whatever percentage your employer matches, contribute that same, if not more, so that you can get that free money from your employer.

3

Hack #3 - Open a Roth IRA

The first two hacks were just scratching the surface on easy ways you can invest, this hack is where we will dive into the very basics of investing into stocks, bonds, ETS, and more. Don't let those words scare you, because this hack will make it so that you don't necessarily have to worry about what you are investing into. Just like the first hack, you would let your money sit and grow.

What is a Roth IRA?

A Roth IRA is a type of retirement account that lets you invest into stocks, bonds, ETS, and more. Since it is a retirement account, you will be able to withdraw the money once you turn 59 ½ with no penalties. Money that is put into a Roth IRA is taxed when you first put it in but won't be taxed once you take it out. In addition, any money that you put in can be withdrawn penalty free. Please note, that although you can withdraw the money you contributed, you cannot withdraw anything else that you earned. An example of this is, if Jen invested $5 and over the course of a week she gained another $5, her total amount now is $10. Jen can take out the $5 she first invested, but cannot take out the full $10 until she retires.

While there is no minimum that you have to contribute, there is a maximum amount every year that you can contribute. This year, 2024, the contribution limit is $7000. After you hit the limit, you can no longer contribute until the next year.

What is the difference between a Traditional IRA and a Roth IRA?

You may have seen something called a Traditional IRA, which is different from a Roth IRA. The main difference between the two is when your money is taxed. In a Traditional IRA, the money you put in is not taxed but once you withdraw it then the money is taxed, whereas with a Roth IRA, the money you put in is taxed, but the money you take out is not taxed. In addition, a Traditional IRA requires you to withdraw a minimum amount of money once you reach a certain age over retirement age. That is not the case with a Roth IRA.

Why you should open a Roth IRA

When I first started my full-time job, I had no idea where to put my hard earned money. I had it all in my checking account, just waiting to be spent. It was only after I opened up a high yield savings account that I finally learned about Roth IRA's. Please note, I recommend you do the first hacks before this one, as this hack I will assume that you have a high yield savings account, and you enrolled into a 401k if your employer provides it.

The first reason why I believe you should open a Roth IRA is because it is an easy way to get into investing. The reason it's so easy is because all you have to do is first open an account, put money into the account, and then choose where to invest. After you do all that, it's just a matter of continuing to contribute and letting your money grow. After I hit the contribution limit on my Roth IRA, I haven't touched it in months and every now and then I check on it and I see that it still grows even if I don't contribute anymore. That is the beauty of investing this way: you don't have to worry about it after you contribute. Your money is working to generate more money while you can spend your time freely.

Another reason why you should open a Roth IRA is because when you contribute and invest money into it, the money that grows will grow tax free so that when you are at the right age to withdraw from it without being penalized, the money will not be taxed since you are already putting in taxed-money into the account from the beginning.

Where to open a Roth IRA

In order to make this simple, I will list just two platforms where you can open up a Roth IRA. I am only listing two as I want this to be as straightforward as possible, and I also know that these two are well known and will be easy to access.

My first recommendation is Fidelity, as I personally use this one myself. Fidelity offers a variety of different accounts that let you invest, and a Roth IRA is the one that I have. The website is very helpful, filled with different information on where to get started, what to look for, and has availability for talking to customer service. I personally followed a guide online on what exactly I needed to do to open an account, so if you are like me and were intimidated by the look and all of the information on the website, I encourage you to also search for a video tutorial online. If not, signing up for an account is very straightforward. You would just need to indicate that you want to open up a retirement IRA, specifically a Roth IRA.

The second place I recommend you open a Roth IRA is with Vanguard. I also use Vanguard for my 401k plan with my employer, and just like Fidelity, it is well known and has been around for a while.

There is no real difference for whichever platform you choose to open up a Roth IRA. The only difference you need to keep in mind are the different ticker symbols both platforms use. Don't worry, I will explain the ticker symbol in the next section.

What to invest in

Once you open up a Roth IRA, link your bank account, and add in some money, then you must be done...right? The answer is, almost! Once you have both of those steps down, it is now time to actually choose where to put your money into to start investing.

The first and most simple place to invest is what's called a Target Date Fund. If you already have a 401k, then most likely you are already investing in this type of fund, so you can skip this if that is the case. If you aren't investing in a Target Date Fund, then this is the perfect place to start. A Target Date Fund is basically a mix of different stocks, bonds, ect. that you can invest in and withdraw once you retire. You can think of it like an all-in-one printer that can photo copy, print, scan, fax, and other fancy stuff. The names of Target Date Funds correlate to the year that you plan to retire. For example, if you are 21 right now in 2024 and plan to retire once you reach 61, then you would look for a Target Date Fund 2085, which represents the year you plan to retire. The ticker symbol, which is a term for the name of a specific stock, will vary if you are using Fidelity or Vanguard. My advice is to simply search up Target

HACK #3 - OPEN A ROTH IRA

Date Fund and the year you plan to retire followed by the platform you are using. You will know instantly which ticker symbol to search for to start investing in it.

The next thing to invest in using Fidelity or Vanguard are index funds. Index funds are a pre-selected number of stocks and bonds that are managed and tracked. This is helpful because instead of choosing which individual stocks or bonds to invest in yourself, an index fund will essentially do all of that for you. The most popular index fund is the S&P 500 Index, which traces the top 500 largest companies. You basically just want to invest in this as it is an easy and low maintenance way to ensure that you are investing your money to grow over time.

4

Hack #4 - Open a Health Savings Account (optional)

If you have followed all of the hacks so far, then congratulations! You have taken the first and easiest steps into investing. For this next hack, it is only available for those Gen Z who are now working full-time with benefits. This is important because a Health Savings Account, or HSA for short, is only eligible to those who have a qualified health plan or health insurance. If you were like me and only enrolled into the most basic and least expensive health plan, then I would double check online and with your HR about your health benefits if you qualify. I also only recommend this next hack to those who have contributed the maximum amount into their Roth IRA, because I believe you would get more out of maximizing your Roth IRA than opening up an HSA before you do so. If this still sounds like something you would like to do, then let's jump into it.

What is an HSA (Health Savings Account)?

An HSA is another type of account that lets you invest money while also being able to use that money to pay for medical expenses both in the present and future. This means that any money that you both put into and invest into this account, you are able to use that money to pay for medical expenses like medications, vaccines, x-rays, and even contact lenses.

Why you should open an HSA

The biggest reason why you should open an HSA is because of the tax benefits that come along with it. The first tax benefit is that while your money is in an HSA, it is not taxed. In addition, any contributions you make can reduce your taxable income, and whenever you withdraw money for medical expenses you will not owe any tax. It is important to note that you must withdraw the money to be used for medical expenses or else these tax advantages will not apply to you. However, once you turn 65, there will be no penalty to withdraw for non medical expenses.

This is important because as you invest, and your money grows, you are able to use that money for medical expenses. And if you have no need for the money at the moment, you can just let it sit there and invest and grow so that in the time you do need it, it is ready for you to withdraw tax free.

5

Hack #5 - Compound Interest is on our side

Now that you have reached this section of the book, it is time to tell you about one of the most important hacks of all. I've mentioned it a few times throughout the book, but there truly is no other ultimate hack than time. As I've said, us Gen Z have time on our side. We have nothing but time, scrolling through social media, posting pictures, buying useless figures for our room, and playing video games. However, it is essential that even if we aren't using this time to do something else that is productive, that if we are just waiting till we wake up in the morning to go to work and then sleep and then repeat, that we need to take advantage of the amount of time we have for our money to grow.

What is Compound Interest?

What I am about to explain may seem very insignificant right now, and that's understandable. Every time we talk about our future and our retirement, it seems like it is so far away. While that may be the case, it is also important to know that time is moving so quickly and before we know it we will be reaching our 40's, looking back on when you were

HACK #5 - COMPOUND INTEREST IS ON OUR SIDE

reading a book about investing for Gen Z.

Compound interest is essentially when you gain interest based on the interest that you have made. Simply put: Interest on interest. What does this look like? Compound interest can best be compared by imagining a small snowball rolling down a hill. As the snowball rolls, it begins to slowly get a little bigger and bigger until it starts to get huge. And the bigger the snowball is, the faster it's going to go down a hill and, in turn, get even bigger. Compound interest is the same way. The snowball represents your money, and as time passes slowly, it will get a little bigger until later, years later, the snowball gets huge and continues to grow because it is going down a hill. This analogy is the best way to explain what compound interest is, because it shows that since we, Gen Z, who are just in their 20's, have money invested, the longer we let it sit the bigger the snowball will be until eventually it will go down the hill to get even bigger.

But don't just take my word for it, simply search up a compound interest calculator online and you can input your own numbers to see how significant this actually is. The only reason we don't really understand the big picture right now is because we are just too young to experience it. I myself just started investing this past year, and although I have gained free money from interest, I have yet to see the true effects of compound interest simply because there hasn't been enough time for it to grow. And us Gen Z have nothing but time now, so take advantage of compound interest and the snowball effect it can have on your money.

6

Hack #6 - Investing in Yourself!

You must have read this last hack and thought to yourself, what do you mean invest in yourself? How does this have anything to do with making more money? To that I ask you, what does this NOT mean? What doesn't this have to do with making more money? It can be easily overlooked but I want you to understand that the biggest investment you can ever make is in yourself.

What does investing in yourself look like?

As someone who has experienced just the first 20ish years of life, I can safely say that I have definitely gone through so much in life and you might be thinking, us Gen Z have barely even experienced half of our life span, how can you be thinking this way? It's simple: I constantly reflect on the different choices and mindsets that I've had from high school to college till now as a young adult just starting to work full-time. Part of that means realizing that I could do so much more with my life. I know that I've repeated over and over that all we do is scroll and scroll, but it comes to a point where we have to really stop and think to ourselves if we could do something more.

HACK #6 - INVESTING IN YOURSELF!

Investing in yourself can look like a number of different things. It can look like you are taking online classes to get a certification. It can look like you are looking up recipes online for a healthier version of a cake you really like. It can even look like you are taking a break, going on a vacation to recharge. The point of investing in yourself is to do something that will benefit yourself in the future. There's no one who can invest in you other than yourself, so it is important to really look at your needs and what you can improve on.

An example that I can give is from my own experience. When I was in my fourth year of college, I was majoring in computer science. I was working hard just like any other student but for some reason, I felt like I was being left behind. My classes were getting progressively harder to understand, my teachers were talking about subjects that they assumed we already knew about, and my classmates seemed like they understood how to do everything. I felt completely alone because I was embarrassed to go to anyone for help. It seemed like I should've known all of this, and when I tried to study on my own I just got even more confused. As the months progressed, I felt stuck in classes that I didn't understand and I didn't want to quit because I already spent years in college. My parents paid for my classes, and I didn't want to disappoint them. I thought that I was investing in my education by taking these classes, but it got to the point where I was getting physically sick due to stress about passing my classes. I eventually dropped out of college and needed to take a reset. At the time, I thought I was a failure for quitting. I thought that I just wasted years of time and money, and that I was the biggest disappointment to my parents for using their money when I had nothing to show for it. However, I now know that the act of dropping college was actually an investment to better myself for the future. There was no way staying in college would've been the investment because I was physically sick, and just continuing classes would've been counterproductive to achieving my goals at the time. I allowed myself to get better, which was the best investment I could've made for myself.

Not only did dropping out of college allow me to go back to my old job, but it also allowed me to have the confidence in myself that I can endure whatever trial I face to bring back a positive outlook on life. Since going back to my old job, I've had 4 promotions with salary increases for all of them. I am now able to fully utilize all of the hacks I've mentioned because of my full-time job, and I constantly look for new opportunities everyday. Investing in yourself will look completely different for each person, but the main thing you want to make sure you do, is to invest in yourself in a way that will benefit you in the long run.

7

Conclusion

If you made it to the conclusion, then congratulations! You can now say that you are an investor and it only goes up from here. In order to make sure you understand all of the points, here is a recap of all of the hacks:

- Hack #1 - Open a High Yield Savings Accounts
- Hack #2 - Contribute to a 401k
- Hack #3 - Open a Roth IRA
- Hack #4 - Open a Health Savings Account (optional)
- Hack #5 - Compound Interest is on our side
- Hack #6 - Investing in Yourself!

Try and remember what all of these mean when you go over them, especially what it means to invest in yourself. Again, these hacks are meant to be simple and easy once you understand how to contribute to them. These hacks allow you to let your money sit and grow on its own, and following these hacks will surely help you invest in your future.

If you found any of these tips helpful, please leave a review on Amazon!

8

References

Cabello, M. (2024, November 4). What is a high-yield savings account? Definition and what to consider. Bankrate. https://www.bankrate.com/banking/what-is-a-high-yield-savings-account/#:~:text=A%20high%2Dyield%20savings%20account%20is%20a%20savings%20account%20that,paying%20upwards%20of%205%20percent

High-Yield Rate:360 Performance Savings | Capital One. (n.d.). Capital One. https://www.capitalone.com/bank/savings-accounts/online-performance-savings-account/nonbrandsem/?gclsrc=aw.ds&gclsrc=aw.ds&gclid=Cj0KCQiAsOq6BhDuARIsAGQ4-zi4XkV1AwEPEI7vEHxPx1QSe13gYY2tbvPg3p6xPy3JH4WSDdU3HSIaAgClEALw_wcB

SoFi. (n.d.). High yield savings account. Retrieved December 13, 2024, from https://www.sofi.com/banking/savings-account/?campaign=MRKT_SEM_MCI_MON_BRAPLUS_ACQ_EXT_ALL_tCPA_E400_20241018_BANKING-SAVINGS-CAL_PSE_GOG_NONE_US_EN_SFv1i284sl58pk08skglr5_e_g_c_719673685595_sofi%20savings&utm_source=MRKT_ADWORDS&utm_medium=SEM&utm_campaign=MRKT_SEM

_MCI_MON_BRAPLUS_ACQ_EXT_ALL_tCPA_E400_20241018_BAN
KING-SAVINGS-CAL_PSE_GOG_NONE_US_EN_SFv1i284sl58pk08sk
glr5_e_g_c_719673685595_sofi%20savings&cl_vend=google&cl_ch
=sem&cl_camp=21824505248&cl_adg=173560419070&cl_crtv=71967
3685595&cl_kw=sofi%20savings&cl_pub=google.com&cl_place=&cl_
dvt=c&cl_pos=&cl_mt=e&cl_gtid=kwd-590669940228&opti_ca=218
24505248&opti_ag=173560419070&opti_ad=719673685595&opti_key
=kwd-590669940228&gclid=Cj0KCQiAsOq6BhDuARIsAGQ4-zhUStlm-
B9ZODkg_jqtnoiToTsHMC7I53rk5v8g2vYEi3XhhHIRGgIaAvn5EALw_
wcB&adname=&gclsrc=aw.ds&gad_source=1&ds_agid=587000088034
91660&ds_cid=71700000120307425&ds_eid=700000001859011&ds_k
id=43700081000100375

High-Yield Savings Account | Western Alliance Bank. (n.d.). https://www.westernalliancebancorporation.com/personal-banking/high-yield-savings-account

Sham, J., & Ayoola, E. (2024, November 19). Roth IRA Basics: What it is, how it works. NerdWallet. https://www.nerdwallet.com/article/investing/what-is-a-roth-ira?utm_source=goog&utm_medium=cpc&utm_campaign=in_mktg_paid_050924_investing_dsa_desktop&utm_term=&utm_content=ta&mktg_hline=19335&mktg_body=2989&mktg_place=dsa-2303771781040&gclsrc=aw.ds&gad_source=1&gclid=Cj0KCQiAsOq6BhDuARIsAGQ4-zjJnEz-0OwcTJ5I5YnO3j6NlywdRBrtun91RD7nR0XZuvOnGosw-P4aAsl0EALw_wcB

Coombes, A., & Sham, J. (2024, November 1). Roth IRA benefits (and drawbacks). NerdWallet. https://www.nerdwallet.com/article/investing/roth-ira-pros-and-cons

Fidelity. (2024, December 10). What's a 401(k)? Retrieved December 13,

REFERENCES

2024, from https://www.fidelity.com/learning-center/smart-money/what-is-a-401k

Fidelity. (2024a, August 14). What is an HSA, and how does it work? Retrieved December 13, 2024, from https://www.fidelity.com/learning-center/smart-money/what-is-an-hsa
  What is compound interest? | Investor.gov. (n.d.). https://www.investor.gov/additional-resources/information/youth/teachers-classroom-resources/what-compound-interest

Chase SavingsSM Account Interest rates | Savings | Chase.com. (n.d.). https://www.chase.com/personal/savings/savings-account/interest-rates

Savings and Certificate of Deposit (CD) interest rates | Wells Fargo. (n.d.). https://www.wellsfargo.com/savings-cds/rates/

Bank of America. (n.d.). Open a Bank of America Advantage Savings account online. https://www.bankofamerica.com/deposits/savings/savings-accounts/

Tierney, S. (2024, February 27). What is APY? Annual Percentage yield Definition and how it works. NerdWallet. https://www.nerdwallet.com/article/banking/what-is-apy

High Yield Savings Account Online with no Fees | Amex US. (n.d.). https://www.americanexpress.com/en-us/banking/online-savings/high-yield-savings-account/?irclickid=_xtsgymz090kfd33wyfxhrb9uzu2xacqz0xwa6m0a00&pext=170911&irgwc=1&extlink=ps2020%3Daffiliate

Fidelity. (2024a, June 25). *How does a 401(k) match work?* Retrieved December 13, 2024, from https://www.fidelity.com/learning-center/smart-money/average-401k-match

Fidelity. (n.d.). *Which IRA is right for you?* Retrieved December 13, 2024, from https://www.fidelity.com/retirement-ira/ira-comparison

Fidelity. (2022, November 29). *What is a target date fund?* Retrieved December 13, 2024, from https://www.fidelity.com/learning-center/personal-finance/what-is-a-target-date-fund

What is an index fund? | Vanguard. (n.d.). https://investor.vanguard.com/investor-resources-education/understanding-investment-types/what-is-an-index-fund

www.ingramcontent.com/pod-product-compliance
Lightning Source LLC
Chambersburg PA
CBHW070944220526
45469CB00007B/2510